Beyond Fairness

Cycle A Gospel Sermons for Proper 13 Through Proper 22

Roy W. Howard

CSS Publishing Company, Inc.
Lima, Ohio

BEYOND FAIRNESS
CYCLE A GOSPEL SERMONS FOR
PROPER 13 THROUGH PROPER 22

FIRST EDITION
Copyright © 2016
by CSS Publishing Co., Inc.

Published by CSS Publishing Company, Inc., Lima, Ohio 45807. All rights reserved. No part of this publication may be reproduced in any manner whatsoever without the prior permission of the publisher, except in the case of brief quotations embodied in critical articles and reviews. Inquiries should be addressed to: CSS Publishing Company, Inc., Permissions Department, 5450 N. Dixie Highway, Lima, Ohio 45807.

Library of Congress Cataloging-in-Publication Data

Names: Howard, Roy, 1954- author.
Title: Beyond fairness : Cycle A gospel sermons for Proper 13 through Proper 22 / Roy Howard.
Description: FIRST EDITION. | Lima : CSS Publishing Company, 2016.
Identifiers: LCCN 2016024783 | ISBN 9780788028380 (alk. paper)
Subjects: LCSH: Bible. Gospels--Sermons. | Sermons, American--21st century. |
Pentecost season--Sermons. | Church year sermons. | Common lectionary (1992). Year A.
Classification: LCC BS2555.54 .H69 2016 | DDC 252/.64--dc23
LC record available at https://lccn.loc.gov/2016024783

For more information about CSS Publishing Company resources, visit our website at www.csspub.com, email us at csr@csspub.com, or call (800) 241-4056.

e-book:
ISBN-13: 978-0-7880-2839-7
ISBN-10: 0-7880-2839-1

ISBN-13: 978-0-7880-2838-0
ISBN-10: 0-7880-2838-3   PRINTED IN USA

*My wife, Claudia, and our daughters,
Rachel and Rebecca, have taught me
to be an honest preacher who
knows what it is to be forgiven.*

*I am grateful for the people of
Saint Mark Presbyterian Church
who have shown me what it
means to welcome all people into
the grace of God.*

Table of Contents

Proper 13 / Pentecost 9 / Ordinary Time 18   7
   You Feed the Hungry
   Matthew 14:13-21

Proper 14 / Pentecost 10 / Ordinary Time 19   13
   Stepping into Liminal Space
   Matthew 14:22-33

Proper 15 / Pentecost 11 / Ordinary Time 20   19
   One Fiesty Woman
   Matthew 15:21-28

Proper 16 / Pentecost 12 / Ordinary Time 21   25
   A Personal Question Deserves a Personal Answer
   Matthew 16:13-17

Proper 17 / Pentecost 13 / Ordinary Time 22   31
   Who Are You Following?
   Matthew 16:21-28

Proper 18 / Pentecost 14 / Ordinary Time 23   37
   The Stop-and-Think Chair
   Matthew 18:15-20

Proper 19 / Pentecost 15 / Ordinary Time 24   43
   House Rules, Forgiveness, and Why Rat Poison
      Is not Good for You
   Matthew 18:21-35

Proper 20 / Pentecost 16 / Ordinary Time 25   49
   Beyond Fairness
   Matthew 20:1-16

Proper 21 / Pentecost 17 / Ordinary Time 26   53
   Words Are not Enough
   Matthew 21:23-32

Proper 22 / Pentecost 18 / Ordinary Time 27   59
   What Are We Protecting?
   Matthew 21:33-46

Pentecost 13 / Proper 9 / Ordinary Time 18
Matthew 14:13-21

You Feed the Hungry

One Friday while Congress was arguing over how to manage the debt crisis, the *Washington Post* drew our attention to another crisis much more severe than the one we were facing as a result of our leaders' inability to find a common ground for the common good. That was bad enough. But much worse was the fact that "more than twelve million people were at risk of death and starvation in the Horn of Africa. Even if they did not perish, young children were likely to suffer the lifelong effect of malnutrition, including poor brain development." Willam Mosely, who wrote the essay, went on to say that the current crisis in Somalia, Kenya, and Ethiopia — the Horn of Africa — was man-made, and not merely the result of drought or climate change. "Just as death from exposure is not an inherent result of cold winter, famine is not a natural consequence of drought. Simply put, the structure of human society often determines who is affected and to what degree." (William G. Moseley, July 29, 2011, *Washington Post*) That was five years ago. Yet, hunger still persists in our world and, in particular, in Africa. But, what's the connection with our text?

We know that food is basic to life; when one is hungry, there is nothing more urgent than satisfying an empty belly. That is why the gospel story of Jesus and the disciples feeding the 5,000 is so instructive.

It began in a lonely place where Jesus had gone to grieve the death of his cousin, John the Baptist. As is so often the case, the crowds found him because they wanted what only he could provide. Watch what Jesus did.

He set aside his own grief, went out to the people, had compassion on them and healed the sick.

When the day was finished, he was exhausted, along with everyone else. This was when things got interesting! The feeding of 5,000 people with a little bread contained the same combination of offering and transformation. Let's look again.

It would have been so much easier at the end of the day for Jesus to have followed the reasonable advice of his reasonable disciples (who undoubtedly were tired and hungry themselves.) The disciples were only trying to be helpful and doing the most reasonable thing possible given the circumstances. They wanted to send the crowds away before it got too late, so they could find shelter and some food in a nearby village. This was not unreasonable advice; after all the disciples had counted up the loaves of bread and took a rough guess at the number of people. One might have said, "You do the math, Jesus, it doesn't add up. Send them away, so you can get some rest too." How can you or anyone else satisfy the hunger of all these people? We would never be as callous — out loud anyway — with the masses wandering across borders in the Horn of Africa.

Jesus didn't send the hungry away. He never does. Undaunted by the magnitude of the need – 5,000 people and only five loaves! — he simply did the compassionate deed with whatever he had at hand. This was the miracle of compassion that his followers were invited to repeat. Take what is at hand — a little of this and a little of that — and give it away to God's hungry people, believing that God will do wonders with our offerings.

Jesus took the small things at hand, like a cup of water and loaf of bread, and did what compassion called for at the moment. He refused to be overwhelmed, either by his own need for comfort or the urgent needs of the people. Instead of experiencing anxiety about not having enough, he looked upon the face of human hunger and did the next right thing. Christians might wonder whether this question will be on the final exam: "What did you do when faced with human hunger?" It seems to me that once again we are faced with that question on the Horn of Africa, and the solution is not simply giving aid although that is certainly one next right step.

Jesus took what was given — five loaves and two fish — and blessed it, offering it to God in gratitude. Then he proceeded to break what was given, so that it could be multiplied. The first action was the taking of what was given, the second was blessing it, then breaking it, and finally giving what was broken that all may have something. Nothing was left behind, and no one was left out. In the end, all were satisfied. How did that happen?

Albert Einstein famously said, "The way I see it, you have two ways to live your life: the one as if no miracles exist and the other as though everything is a miracle." To be open to the miraculous is to be open to impossible things becoming possible. It is a stance toward life that is fundamentally hopeful. One that places confidence in God always and is especially confident when all other sources have run out. Einstein's comment begs the question, what is a miracle?

When the IRA issued an apology for its history of violence, commentators described it as a miracle. Was it? A mother asked a well-known preacher to make her disabled daughter walk again. When the pastor replied, "I can't," the mother said, "Well what good are you?" In the search for a physical change, she dismissed the miracle of life in the relationship itself. Just what is a miracle?

Each of these instances, even the one rejected, contains some human offering that can be transformed into something beyond what was thought possible. An offering of ourselves becomes the vehicle for the miraculous to occur. I suspect something of the miraculous is needed across the whole world, among the vast numbers of displaced persons, not to mention Capitol Hill.

Did the miracle in the gospel occur, as Barbara Brown Taylor suggested, when the meager basket of bread and fish was passed among the people and they dug into their pockets to add the secret bit of bread they had brought along the journey? By the time the baskets had been passed around, had people taken enough to eat, but also put a little back in to share with others because that seemed like the only right thing to do?

I don't know how miracles occur, but the gospel tells us that when the faithful act boldly, sharing our resources with others, miraculous things begin to happen. When people trust in God and act with compassion, scarcity can and often is transformed into abundance.

We might take this a step further and call this the Eucharistic life of taking what is given — the whole of our lives, blessing it — the joys, frustrations, and sorrows alike, breaking it — allowing ourselves to be broken open in compassion and sharing the pieces — offering our lives and our gifts to others.

But there is more to the story. The human body can exist for only so long without food. Yet, we know that material abundance is not enough. There are other hungers that are as urgent. In each of us, there is a hunger for connection, for meaning, for beauty, and for love.

Saint Augustine believed that underneath all human hungers is a desire for God. "Our hearts are restless until we find our rest in thee," he prayed. The temptation is to satiate ourselves with junk foods — quick-fix superficial relationships, endless entertainment, consumerism — that keep us going, even transform (or malform) us, but cannot satisfy the deepest yearnings of our hearts for God.

Nowhere is the generosity of God's love shown more clearly than at the Lord's table where the hungry children of God are fed. There we relive Christ's actions when he took the bread, blessed it, broke it, and gave it to the disciples to share with the hungry. We are invited to do the same. Our actions in the world addressing the hungry flow directly from God's action toward us in the Eucharist. No wonder Calvin wanted a weekly service of Holy Communion.

We might consider the same knowing that the hungry still gather around the Lord's table with open hands and open hearts, remembering that Jesus never turned the hungry away. He fed them generously until all were satisfied. No junk food — he is bread of life, given that all may have life.

Alleluia. Amen.

Proper 14 / Pentecost 10 / Ordinary Time 19
Matthew 14:22-33

Stepping into Liminal Space

When Peter stepped out of that boat, he stepped into liminal space to walk on water. Some of you may be wondering what is liminal space?

Liminal space is a term used by cultural anthropologists to describe in-between or transitional passages of communities. It describes those times when the past is no longer sustainable, and the future is not yet clear. The present is a time of unsettledness, unable to rely on the past and unsure about the future. There are some who are sure that the United States is in liminal space, making a transition toward a new, yet unknown future. I believe that's true. Taking this further the psychologist Carl Jung applied the concept of liminality to people, not just cultures. Jung described liminality as the emotional space where the present situation no longer satisfies, but the future to which one is heading is not yet clear. The moment one steps from a familiar situation toward an unfamiliar, you enter liminal space.

For example, this can happen to someone who moves from a well-defined religion, filled with ready answers that once satisfied but no longer work, toward an embrace of God whose ways are not our ways. It can happen to a young person leaving home for college, or a mother re-entering the workplace after being away for years to raise children. In each instance, you are no longer in the familiar but not satisfying place, but neither are you in the new situation yet. Liminality is an unsettling, disorienting transitional space. Here's the crucial point: Jung believed the experience of such disorientation and disturbance to be essential for emotional wholeness.

Now back to Peter and his experience of liminal space.

He was in that boat in a stormy sea, along with his friends. He was a fisherman who must have been familiar with stormy seas even at night. But he was not familiar with what appeared on the horizon at early dawn. In the distance, a ghostlike figure loomed, which frightened everyone. That figure, sensing their fear, tried to calm them with his familiar words: "Be encouraged, fear not. I am with you." Peter somehow sensed the presence of the Lord. We don't know how these things happened: sensing the presence of God. In response to Peter's inquiry, Jesus invited him to come. Just come. That's all.

Peter knew nothing except the one who was calling him to do the impossible. Isn't this a short summary of faith: responding to the call of God however one hears it? Peter did just that. Summoned by the Lord, he stepped away from every known support, every familiar structure, and acting solely on faith, he walked into liminal space toward the Lord who was calling. Notice that he was focused not on himself or his abilities; he was focused on God made manifest in Jesus Christ. He was utterly disoriented in the grip of radical faith, on the way toward a new orientation, one that would be determined by this mysterious God who calls. For an astonishing moment that must have seemed a lifetime, Peter was suspended in faith with his gaze fixed solely on the one who is calling.

Then it happened. His doubts overcame his faith, his gaze shifted toward himself doing the impossible and, of course, left to his own devices, he knew he was sunk; or at least sinking fast, only to be saved by the one who graciously called him into a new orientation.

If you do not believe this literally happened, it need not take away from the power of this story to describe the life of faith. This is the way of life that the followers of Christ are summoned to: knowing nothing except the one who is calling us toward him. This is true faith and of course it's frightening. Remember all liminal space is disorienting and disturbing because you are not fully in control. Yet whenever you refuse to let fear determine the future, and instead risk following Christ's call, astonishing things occur. We are not overcome by fear because we know the one who is calling is the one who saves us. The life of faith means always living in liminal space — cultivating the capacity of heart to hear Christ's invitation in our lives, and hearing that invitation, stepping out of comfortable, yet unsatisfying structures toward a future that only God knows. This is the journey that we together are walking in faith. Once we grasp that Peter did not drown and neither will we, then a wild freedom begins.

In a similar way the people of Israel, having been freed from slavery and sent on their way to the promise land, found themselves in the wilderness. They were in liminal space — neither in the past, which was familiar though harsh, nor in the future toward which they were heading. Rather they were in that disorienting place where all faith in God is formed. Once in the wilderness, they complained against their leaders. Moses, Aaron: send us back to what is familiar! We hated it, but at least it was familiar. Out here we are going to die.

The people of Israel faced an adaptive challenge. In that in-between place of faith, the community — just like the church — has to find ways to adapt creatively to the challenges of their situation. They are disoriented in liminal space on the way to new orientation in a new land, being formed as a free people who will radically depend upon God. Again, fear threatens to overwhelm them, even to the point of wanting to go back to slavery.

Adaptive challenges are rarely easy, but they actually bring out the best in a people when embraced. They require creative responses, patience, and faith in an unsettled time. Getting to the promised land is not a straight line. Leaders are hard pressed to not give in to fear and the demands that go with it. The same is true for our elected leaders, public servants, who are leading our society at this crucial liminal time. The people complained, "We will die out here!" The same complaint is heard today. In fact, they may be right; society as we know it may die, and we don't yet know what will replace it. But we do know it will not serve us well if our public leaders give in to fear and lead us back to what is familiar. That may "feel good" but in the end it may be the opposite direction toward which we need to move if we are to be renewed for the economic and political challenges we face.

It's easy to forget that the role of spiritual leaders in a community is to name the theological issue at the core of an adaptive challenge. Moses and Aaron, sorely tested leaders, direct the attention of the people to God. It's against God that you are complaining. Your fear has overwhelmed your faith in the one who has brought us this far and will bring us home one day. Take it up with God. The core theological issue in this adaptive challenge is faith in God, whose ways are not our ways and whose mystery is inscrutable, yet always merciful and kind.

We are living with other adaptive challenges. How are we to proclaim afresh the good news of God's love to people awash in a sea of bad news, desperate to hear good news? When people look upon the church as a haven for pedophiles and greedy egomaniacs, how do we speak a word of saving grace? In so many ways the larger church in our time is in liminal space, in-between there and then, often disoriented on the way to something new, not yet revealed. Yet facing an unknown and frightening future, we are a people of faith, who trust not in our own abilities, but like Peter, have fixed our eyes upon Jesus Christ who summons us into a new orientation.

Jesus said, "Fear not! Be of good courage!" Come to this feast of forgiveness — the table of the Lord in the wilderness — where the provisions are plentiful for the journey ahead.

Amen.

Proper 15 / Pentecost 11 / Ordinary Time 20
Matthew 15:21-28

One Fiesty Woman

We could begin by noting that this is one fiesty woman. Or, at the risk of irreverence, we could begin by noting that Jesus is one rude man. Rather than focus on one or the other, I suggest we explore the relationship enfolded in this remarkable gospel story and then ask about the implications for us.

That the encounter between Jesus, the Jew, and this woman, a Gentile, even occurred was remarkable enough, but the fact that Matthew chose to tell it, and not erase it from history, makes it astounding. After all, this woman was not just any Gentile, she was a Canaanite, and as such represented a despised, indigenous rural population with whom Jews were forbidden to associate. Yet she, the despised outsider, addressed Jesus as "Lord, Son of David," and revealed herself to be a believer, and not merely a pagan from Canaan. That in itself is worth noting.

But what about Jesus? His initial reaction was so offensive that some have argued that it didn't happen. It was planted by Jewish Christians who didn't approve of the church's mission to the Gentiles, but Gentile Christians later added the happy ending to prove their point. Then there are those who want to clean up the story by claiming that when Jesus referred to dogs, he was using the Arabic diminutive that means he was referring to household pets, like a term of endearment. Some say that he was merely testing the woman's faith, as if that makes his behavior any better.

I say hogwash! to both. They are misguided attempts to defang the gospel story by ignoring Christ's humanity and dismissing the life-changing power of faith that dares to take risks for the sake of those who suffer. All attempts to domesticate the gospel so that it conforms to our expectations render it a sentimental tale with little power to influence our lives or change the world. The same can be said about all attempts to domesticate Jesus. Instead, I suggest accepting the story as it is, with its rough, rude edges, listening carefully for what Jesus revealed about God and what this fiesty, pagan woman revealed about the nature of faith. Biblical scholars insist that the more difficult the story, the more likely it was historically true. Why? Because if one was to make up a story about Jesus, it is much more likely to be one that presented him in a positive light. This one does not, at least not on the first glance.

Perhaps, you'll remember the film version of *The Last Temptation of Christ*. It was nearly as controversial as Mel Gibson's *The Passion of the Christ*, but for different reasons. The film, and the novel, focus intensely on the humanity of Jesus, suggesting that Jesus, before accepting the cross of redemption, fantasized about being married, having children, and living out his days with his family in the country. It was all a dream, but the mere suggestion that Jesus might have entertained such thoughts at the hour of his crucifixion scandalized millions of people, including believing Christians.

Why be offended by the humanity of Jesus? The Christian faith has always taught that Jesus was fully human and fully divine, and that has been a struggle for some, from the very beginning. If we believe that Jesus was indeed fully human, then we can assume he passed through all the trials of every human being. He laughed and he cried; in fact, nowhere was his humanity more poignantly revealed than when his dear friend Lazarus died. Jesus wept. He lashed out in anger at the injustice of religious leaders. He suffered emotional torment in the garden. And here, in this surprising encounter with a despised indigenous woman, Jesus revealed his initial narrow understanding of his full vocation. Acknowledging the full humanity of Jesus allows us to marvel even more with wonder and gratitude at the full divinity of Jesus whose love was displayed for all. In the end, it was a woman — a religious outsider — who opened his heart to the fullness of his divine vocation.

She pleaded not for herself but for her tormented, suffering daughter. Initially, Jesus ignored her. But, she would not be deterred. She, the outsider, knew who he was even more clearly than he did at that moment. Though she called him by the familiar Jewish phrase, "Lord, Son of David," she knew that he was Lord of the universe, unrestrained by ancient boundaries. Her pleading turned to screaming. Isn't that appropriate for a mother heartbroken by her child's suffering?

When someone is suffering, it is not the time to be meek and mild, polite in prayer, as if there was nothing at stake in the venture. No, true prayer involves the risk of authentic, honest expression. Anything less is hardly worth the effort. The natural outcome of prayer is compassion for the other. Prayer that remains isolated from the suffering can too easily become a spiritual exercise of self-indulgence. On the other hand, prayer that boldly dares to intercede for the suffering person not only draws one closer to God, but it opens the heart in deep solidarity with the one who is hurting. This is true prayer.

The disciples, threatened by this outrageous display of dangerous, risk-taking prayer, urged Jesus to send her away. Dismiss her with all the other pagan outsiders, they said. Jesus started to follow their misguided advice, insisting that his mission was singly focused on the lost sheep of Israel. But the woman knew Jesus better than he knew himself. Once she had his attention, she was not going to let go.

If it is true that faith is a verb, not merely a noun, then this Canaanite woman displayed fully what this means in practice. Even when Jesus tried again to dismiss her with a rude proverb about children and dogs, she continued her banter, insisting that even dogs get the crumbs that fall from the table. We cringe at the dialogue, but what was important was the radical, risky faith of this woman on behalf of the suffering one. At the end of the day, this kind of faith was precisely what finally captured Jesus' imagination, cracked open his heart, and revealed his true divine vocation that stretched to embrace everyone.

Wide-eyed and apparently stunned by it all, Jesus was a human being utterly transformed by this encounter. Can you see that? He began ignoring her and ended by praising her. Her faith summoned forth his divine healing, and in an instant, the barrier between insiders and outsiders was demolished. She went on her way, the demons fled from her suffering daughter, and once more, we get a glimpse of Jesus' true vocation.

How about you and me? Is there anything in your life that you want to be certain you bring fully before God in prayer? Will you risk being tenacious, fierce, and fiesty before God in the confidence that God is worthy of all your prayer and desire? It would be so much easier to let go of our desires, our needs, and our hopes for the other in the face of what appears to be silence from God. Our prayers seemingly go unanswered, and we walk away in silence. Perhaps that is to give up all too easily.

It is also much too common to look upon ourselves and believe that we are unworthy to ask God for anything, much less to ask for the very thing that will help another. We start to believe the lies that undermine our faith and well-being. We believe the gifts of God come to those who deserve them, and we certainly aren't among the deserving crowd.

Then we might wonder if the risk of being fully vulnerable before the Lord with all our fierce desires for what is good for another is just too difficult. Vulnerability requires a level of courage and faith that is much more demanding of us than merely being content with our religious life without ever really stepping fully into a live relationship with the Lord Jesus in prayer.

The encounter with Jesus and this woman teaches us a different way. She dared to be vulnerable with her deepest desires, undeterred by the power of shame or those who were scandalized by her raw requests. She showed us courage before the Lord, and in showing us courage, she also showed us a quality of faith that opened the heart of our Lord. What is even more remarkable is that this woman was an outsider to the faith. Are our eyes and ears open to learn from the outsider about faith and courage?

This fiesty Canaanite woman teaches us to be daring in prayer, relentless in pleading the cause of the suffering, and faithful in believing that one day the demons who torment the wounded will flee and in Jesus, healing will happen.

Let those who have ears to hear, hear. Amen.

Proper 16 / Pentecost 12 / Ordinary Time 21
Matthew 16:13-17

A Personal Question Deserves a Personal Answer

One warm August night and only two of us standing on our neighbor's deck. The others had gone inside to escape the heat and eat the dessert waiting in the cool kitchen. Alone on the deck in the descending darkness of early evening my neighbor asked, "So, how did you find the Lord?" It was not a question I was expecting at a neighborhood dinner party, or any party for that matter, where politics, religion, and conviviality don't mingle with one another. It made me uncomfortable and slightly embarrassed. Honestly, my first thought was that he might have had too much to drink and was just teasing his neighbor, the Reverend, as he refers to me. Then I looked at his face and knew he was serious, whether drunk or not. His question was about more than me. In the uncluttered directness of that moment, alone on the deck, my neighbor was asking a personal question that may have been as much about him as it was about me. He was asking an honest question and not just having fun mocking a Christian. What could I say? A direct question deserved a direct answer, and in this case, a personal answer, not a general religious one. He wanted something from real not religious; something from the heart not only the head.

I wonder if the encounter between Jesus and Peter was similar. Jesus asking Peter, "Who do you say that I am?" was a personal question to which Jesus expected a personal answer and not an answer that merely echoed what the general public was saying. He knew what others were saying about him. Jesus wanted to know where Peter stood in relation to him. But I wonder whether Jesus, like my neighbor, was asking the question for himself as much as for Peter. Was he looking for Peter to confirm in him what he knew to be true, but wanted Peter to know it, too? It's a poignant moment. Peter was compelled to give a straight answer to Jesus' question. It was his way of saying: get real with me.

When my neighbor asked how I found the Lord, I could have easily dismissed him and suggested we head for the dessert table. He wasn't interested in dessert. So I decided to get real with him; I decided to give him an honest answer.

I told him that it made more sense to describe how God found me, rather than me finding the Lord. After all, the Lord wasn't lost, so why should I talk about finding him, as if I were the hero of the story? I told my friend that though the Lord wasn't lost, I surely was, even though I was the coolest kid on the block. I would rather talk about the goodness of the shepherd who never ceases looking for lost ones, including this one who had drifted away from the church at a tender age because the church seemed more concerned for its own survival than anything else. As best I could tell at that time, the church was either clueless or not interested in addressing the issues that were rocking my world, including where God was when everything else was falling apart.

Having abandoned a church that seemed capable of endless talking and a myriad of activities, but never a compelling word of God in the midst of war, racism, class division, and basic social breakdown, I was left to search on my own, along with thousands of others in my generation. While the church of my youth was doing reasonably fine, carrying on its civic club activities that mirrored every other all-white, do-good, social club ensuring the continuation of a stable, American Protestant civil religion for at least a few more years, thousands of people like me were happily adrift, protesting this war and that action, sampling this drug or another, singing of freedom without any spiritual mooring, and desperately searching for something called home for the heart.

I told my neighbor that Jesus, the Good Shepherd, finally found me when a couple of people from the church that I had abandoned as hopeless, asked me if I wanted to enter into a life with Jesus, who forgives sins and gives to all who follow him abundant life. Rather than laugh at them or ridicule them as I expected to do when I opened the door, I heard in their simple invitation something true and honest. I wanted to laugh at them, but something else happened. I didn't walk away. Instead I heard an invitation to come home. As I have learned over the years since that time, they were giving me an opportunity to enter a lifelong journey of discipleship in the Christian faith that begins with a personal commitment to follow Jesus, the Good Shepherd, who searches relentlessly for the lost until all are brought home.

It seems to me that the Christian life begins and ends with the personal knowledge that one is found by a gracious God. The consequence of the astonishing good news of being found is the desire to live his ways in your life. I realize that the fears of being mistaken for a fundamentalist (horror!) have made it awkward for many of us to put it this way; nevertheless, there is an undeniable personal commitment that is at the heart of Christianity. When Jesus asked Peter, "Who do you say that I am?" he was asking about his allegiance to him not about his general religious knowledge. When you declare Jesus to be the incarnation of God, you are declaring your own place in the universe of spiritual beliefs and practices. Without such a commitment it is all too easy to construct your own religion that leaves you at some distance from the living God. That distance is the definition of lost. Strange as it may sound, it is possible to be lost without even knowing it until someone asks you to get real.

Again, strangely enough, one can maintain membership in religious institutions and engage in religious activities, even use religious language, "God talk," but have no personal allegiance to any God, including the one known in Jesus. That is how we end up with American Christendom: religion without discipleship or where nothing personal is at stake. When the chips are gone and the ship of state is sinking, it is only self that matters. That is a very small island on which to rest one's life.

Religion is easy, following Jesus is not. That is the truth that Jesus was after when he asked Peter to get real. It's what he is after when he asks us to get real and follow him.

That hot August night, I told my neighbor, when those slightly odd church people came to my door to offer me an opportunity to follow Jesus, I said yes, even though I was not at all sure what I was doing, only that I had a sense I was no longer alone and that I was somehow coming home to the community that I had abandoned so many years earlier. In order to be found, I had to admit that I was lost. I was caught up in a world that could never satisfy no matter how comfortable it seemed to be. No one can be found who does not finally admit to being lost. I was and I did. It's not to say that I have never felt again the bewildering absence of God or awakened with the fears of being lost on my own.

My slightly tipsy neighbor didn't ask if that meant that everything is okay with me, but I told him anyway. I stumble more often than walk, I fail more often than follow, I'm more like Peter than Paul, and I believe, despite my doubt, that the one in whom I have put my trust is faithful and will not abandon me. As Saint Paul says, whether we live or die, we belong to the Lord. For that I am grateful.

Jesus is not any easier to follow, in fact, as I get older and more comfortable and as the world continues to be wracked by war and poverty, it is more difficult to walk in his way. Then and now, Jesus does not offer an easy way, so that I might be better adjusted to this ungodly world of war, greed, violence, and deception. He calls me, as he called Peter, to let go of my own life so that I might enter into his life that counters this world, and in him find peace. "Who do you say that I am?" is the question that invites me over and over again to cling to Christ who is my only hope.

So, friends, beloved of God, let me ask you a personal question. It's time to get real. How is it that God found you?

Amen.

Proper 17 / Pentecost 13 / Ordinary Time 22
Matthew 16:21-28

Who Are You Following?

"If any want to be my followers, let them deny themselves, take their cross and follow me." The first thing that needs to be said is that this is a difficult teaching of Jesus. We should not fool ourselves. It's better to confess this at the beginning than to pretend otherwise and lose our way in the end. The honesty with which we hold our lives before God is the measure of our desire to be followers of Jesus and not merely religious spectators. The second thing that needs to be said is that it's the end of our lives that Jesus is concerned about in this teaching. The end not as the last moment, but the end as in *the goal* of our lives. When the old Westminster catechism asks, "What is the chief end of man?" it wants us to consider, "What is the primary purpose of human life?" The answer is worth remembering: "The chief end of humanity is to glorify God and enjoy God forever." What is our primary purpose in life, and how will we arrange everything around that purpose?

At this point Jesus had come to the moment when he needed to be as clear as possible with his disciples about the way of life that was before them. Dietrich Bonhoeffer famously called this "the cost of discipleship" and cautioned that it was not cheap.

Do you remember playing Follow the Leader? Of course, you do! The rules are simple. The leader gets to go wherever she chooses, and the followers either follow or quit the game. Followers don't get to tell the leader where to go, that's her choice alone. With my gang of friends, we'd march into the woods or down an unknown path, across a new neighborhood or through an alley; the leader leads and the choice is always there. Every follower continually decides how far he will go with whoever is leader, especially when she goes in way that is scary. If you are following, it's always a matter of trust and choice.

Christians are playing Follow the Leader, only the game is life and it never actually ends, except in death, unless we walk away and refuse to play any longer. Jesus is continually saying, "Follow me, and I will lead you in the way that leads to life." Along this way you will lose what this world tells you is most important, and in the end, you will discover your real life, and that's really important!

We play this game all our lives in one way or another, whether we acknowledge it or not, it's a game of trust and choice. For the followers of Jesus the choice is always before us. How far will you follow him when the path leads along a way that you don't yet know or understand? How much do you trust the one you are following? Peter couldn't fathom that his leader would go the way of suffering. He resisted mightily. His trust was tested by the way of the cross that Jesus set before him.

In the children's game, the leader realizes that if your followers don't trust you, the game will end quickly. The followers will walk away. Jesus experienced that, and the same is true in our lives. Only our lives are never truly over until our baptism is made complete in death. The real question becomes: Who am I following? What path am I on? Do I have faith in the one whose way I am walking? It may seem irreverent to call this a game because games are fun and silly. But even though this game is not silly and certainly not always fun, it will bring you to the deepest joy of all: discovering God's purpose.

So we are back at the opening confession: this is a difficult teaching. We find it strange to walk in the way of Christ.

It leads you away from self-preservation to the cross where your life is given away for the sake of others. This is not a path that we ordinarily follow. We follow a way that protects us; Jesus followed a way that led to vulnerability. Yet he promised that as we develop the capacity to trust him, becoming vulnerable, we will actually find our heart's desire: life abundant. Here we might summon our hearts to sing the old gospel song: "Trust and obey, for there's no other way to be happy in Jesus, but to trust and obey."

We have now come to the point where we meet the true meaning of the cross, when we might desperately want the game to be over. Can I get back to the normal life where I am in control, the one where I get to be the leader? Our normal way is to hold on to the things that we want, while Jesus, our leader, takes us on a path that requires giving up what we want for the sake of what God wants for our lives.

Discovering what God desires and orienting our lives in that direction is the way of the cross. It will likely mean personal sacrifice, inconvenience, and vulnerability.

Sören Kierkegaard once said that there are more admirers of Christ than followers of Jesus. You can admire Christ easily and still go on with church activities. You can come to worship and feel morally chastised, or pleasantly uplifted and go home satisfied, only to return to life as it always has been with nothing changed; still admiring Christ. The choice is whether we will seek to be disciples being changed by faith decisions, or be content to be an admirer of Christ.

For instance, James Emery White, the pastor of Mecklenburg Community Church in Charlotte, North Carolina, has spoken out widely on the dangers of sports eclipsing family life. To his thriving, vital congregation of young families he said, "Let's say this out loud, in front of the mirror, and see if we like it: 'I will do spiritual things for my child's sake until sports conflict, then sports win.' " For White, and many parents, that uncomfortable choice is a *cross* moment.

If it all seems confusing and too demanding, you are in good company. The disciples thought the same thing, especially Peter. This is pretty hard stuff. But Jesus didn't intend it to be so hard for us to understand. I think he wanted his followers to know something rather simple. He was going to die so that others may live. This is the meaning of the cross.

It is a paradoxical way whereby losing means gaining, and dying means living. Becoming vulnerable means becoming courageous. This is so counterintuitive that we often miss it. The more we embrace the way of the cross and the more we open ourselves to God's love, the more we discover joy and abundance.

Following Jesus is a way of life that is shaped by letting go. It is to find life at its most purposeful when you are giving your life away. It is offering your cloak to the man who has none, walking the second mile when one seems enough, or turning the other cheek when it appears so much smarter to retaliate. This is where we get confused; it is by choosing to die to the things that we take as "common sense" that we find joy in this mortal life.

A good leader tells the truth. Jesus told his followers to watch out: you can gain the whole world and lose your soul. It's a kind word of caution that we need to hear, because we are surrounded by messages that say otherwise. You can gain all sorts of stuff, power, and prestige, and realize you are empty, still looking for what satisfies the soul.

For the followers of Jesus the way leads to a cross. He told us that honestly, but he also told us as we learn to walk in his way, we will find life abundant. We cannot follow this way in our own strength, and if we could, we would only end up with the delusion of power and self-preservation, isolated from others.

There is a better way. It's the way of the cross. It's a game in which the goal is God's purpose for your life and living into that purpose.

It's the way of faith, trusting not in your capacity to get it right or always do it well, but trusting in the one you are following.

It's by following that we learn to follow. We learn to walk by walking. We become courageous by being vulnerable. We find life by letting go of life only to find God's life given back to us. It's a strange and wonderful way that Jesus sets before us.

We all follow someone. We all play the game.

In the end it comes down to this: who are you going to follow?

Amen.

Proper 18 / Pentecost 14 / Ordinary Time 23
Matthew 18:15-20

The Stop-and-Think Chair

Schools opened here last week, and I remembered something from one of the teachers. Like all good teachers, she has certain expectations — norms of behavior — for her students. The students agree to these community norms for the classroom that are posted in the room. That's not new. What I find intriguing in her classroom is the consequence if someone breaks the norm. When a community rule is broken, the offending student is assigned to the clearly labeled *stop-and-think* chair. There the child sits ruminating upon certain actions and considering what he or she needs to do to return to the classroom community. I wonder if that would work in other settings — like the nation's capitol or home and yes, the church. It's a silly thought, but still. Imagine if all communities — even, or especially, those where there is so much blood being shed against one another, so much violence flowing out of their lives — imagine if all communities had a public spot designated for the *stop-and-think* chair. You've heard of stop, drop, and roll in a fire? How about stop, think, and pray in a conflict? You don't have to be humiliated with a dunce cap; just stop and think.

When we allow for a moment of reflection, it often provides enough space for consideration of another path. Such silence becomes a container for the Spirit of God to intervene in surprising ways.

I remember when a friend came to speak to me about something I had done to him. He began speaking firmly and kindly, as a friend and not an enemy, which certainly helped me to hear him without defense. As he was speaking clearly from his heart, I sensed my own heart being pierced. There was nothing to say in defense, for what he said was true, although I don't think I would have come to that conclusion on my own. It took a friend, a brother in Christ, to reveal my blind spot. I wish I had a *stop-and-think* chair and a prayer closet for my exposed soul.

It was a difficult conversation for both of us. Being vulnerable with one another is often that way. Yet it is only by stepping into the discomfort that you can ever step out of it. Speaking honestly is uncomfortable because you risk missing the log in your own eye while focusing on the splinter in the other's eye. One can easily slip from a just complaint to being just judgmental. For me it was difficult and uncomfortable to say the least, because hearing one's own offense shatters self-pretensions. Who doesn't cling to some illusions about the self? So it was a difficult and demanding conversation. Truth telling brings light to every corner of our hearts. Truth shatters illusions. That's painful, but that's not all.

Here is the thing about becoming vulnerable, speaking honestly, and listening nondefensively: it is painful, but it is also deeply healing. For some people it can be transformative. It remains so for me. Even though my offense was not large in the grand scale of sins — no adultery, murder, extortion, bribery; not even gossip, innuendo, slander, deception, and backbiting — these are the standard sins of our culture. The scale of the offense doesn't matter.

In Matthew's gospel, it's the healing of the heart and transformation of our lives that Jesus is after when he tells his followers to care enough to confront the one who sins against his brother or sister.

That's why I'm glad my friend spoke to me. He helped me recognize where our relationship had been broken and to set out on a new way. When the truth compels one to begin a new way, the gospel calls it salvation. It is a gift of God, just as repentance is a gift of grace, not some grit-your-teeth penitential exercise. The good news is that God gives this gift to those who hear the truth and open their hearts to a new way of life.

Here's more good news: my brother in Christ is still my best friend on the planet. We have spoken honestly to one another now for years. That friendship is one of the finest gifts of my life. I doubt I could say that today if he had not spoken so honestly and so kindly years ago.

If we lived in a perfect world, with perfect families, marriages, friendships, communities, and congregations there would be no need for such truth telling. But that is not the world we live in, nor was it for Jesus and the early communities of his followers. If it were there would be no need for Matthew to record these guidelines for how Christians are to handle offenses when they occur among us. It's Matthew's version of the *stop-and-think* chair.

After years of serving the church in a variety of settings and congregations for nearly 25 years, I've come to the conclusion that we tolerate a whole lot of bad behavior — what the gospel calls sin — rather than taking the hard way of honest speech aimed at repentance and restoration. This tolerance for bad behavior is not because of humility, love, and forbearance. It's because of the failure to care enough to hold people accountable for their behavior and the lack of agreement on community norms. Whenever bad behavior is tolerated, the whole community is mocked. Many people steer a wide path away from churches because of the bad behavior that goes unchecked and unaccounted for by the participants. They don't want any part of it.

I think it is similar to other relationships in our lives. A marriage that tolerates abusive behavior has no life. A family that allows bad behavior without a structure for respect and love is bound for disaster. When I was growing up, children out-of-control — which means bad behavior unchecked by a *stop-and-think* chair — were often called "little monsters." That is an apt description of the havoc that occurs in families without boundaries or rules of discipline.

Family life is not much different from congregational life. They are remarkably similar. Matthew knows this. He knows that people can and will sin against one another. People will, in fact, act like "little monsters." Little monsters may be too polite a description for the people whose unchecked violence is spilling out all over the world. For the sake of the health of the community — family, friendship, congress, country, and congregation — there must be rules of discipline and people faithful enough to speak honestly. Just as in family life, the goal is not merely punishment much less banishment, but change toward a new way of living. A friend of mine told his out-of-control, young-adult son that he must leave his home because the family could no longer tolerate his actions. It was the hardest thing he has ever done in his life. He did it in the hope that it will clear a path for a new life yet to be. When honesty leads to a new way of life that is called salvation. And that is the deep hope for us all.

The gospel teaches us that the way of love is hard for the followers of Jesus. Yet, just as in family life or the classroom, tolerating offenses or even rewarding them by silence serves no good purpose. Matthew teaches that tolerating bad behavior, which is a form of reward, actually destroys the health of the whole community. That is true everywhere, in every form of community.

Sometimes the way of love is hard. That's true. Gregory Jones says, "We need to acknowledge the intense pain, anger, and bitterness that exist for people who have suffered and continue to suffer the effects of sin and evil in our world. Cultivating a practice of reconciling forgiveness takes time, a creative reclamation of the understanding of sin and forgiveness.... Reconciling forgiveness is not easy; it is costly.

It is not quick; it is a lifelong struggle. It is not a commodity; it is the investment of the entirety of our lives. Perhaps the first thing the contemporary church — across the traditions — needs to do is confess to God our failures to be genuinely a confessing church, to sustain communities of reconciling forgiveness."[1]

Sentimentality is easy and many people follow that path. Love is hard. But it's also true that Jesus — the living Christ — promises to be with us every step of the way. That is the good news. At the Lord's table we see the visible expression of our vulnerable God whose way is reconciliation and peace. Here we see an alternative way: The way of sharing and the way a community learns forgiveness.

We come hungry to the feast of forgiveness that the Lord has graciously set for us. He feeds us with the Bread of Life and cup of our salvation. Alleluia!

Amen.

---

1. L. Gregory Jones, *Embodying Forgiveness: A Theological Analysis* (Grand Rapids: Wm. B. Eerdmans Publishing Company, 1995).

Proper 19 / Pentecost 15 / Ordinary Time 24
Matthew 18:21-35

House Rules, Forgiveness, and Why Rat Poison Is not Good for You

I have two public school elementary teachers in my family. I've learned a great deal about what goes on behind the scenes long before the students arrive and long after they have left: the seating chart, the reading corner, the attractive posters, imaginative strategies for teaching difficult concepts, and much more. There is a lot to teaching. The same can be said for those people who teach congregations of every size every Sunday. There is so much that happens behind the scenes from Monday to Saturday night in preparation for Sunday morning, so that others may learn about and experience the goodness of God in Jesus Christ. It's really quite amazing. I am pretty sure we don't offer enough gratitude for Sunday school teachers all over the church. One of my favorite bumper stickers remains: "Have you thanked a teacher today?"

When I asked a new public school teacher what's the most important thing on the first day of school she said, without hesitation, "Setting the common rules for the classroom. That creates the tone for the whole year, in one day." Then she went through a list of the expectations for classroom conduct: respect one another, one person talks at a time, raise your hand, be kind to one another, be prepared, be on time, and so on. "It's so important," she said, "to establish common ground for discipline as soon as possible. If you don't get agreement on that, or you lose it, it's crazy — just about impossible."

I once spent several weeks at St. Benedict's Monastery in Snowmass, Colorado. As in all the Benedictine monastic communities, the monks are guided by the *Rule of Saint Benedict*, a book written in the sixth century to provide structure and discipline to the community. It is drenched in scripture. The beauty of the rule is actually quite similar to the classroom. When life together breaks down, as it always does, there is an objective guide for the monks to follow. Abuse of power is restrained by the rule. Life flows in the monastery purposefully, as it does in a classroom — not without bumps and disagreements, of course, but with a common structure to handle them when they occur. Like the well-ordered classroom, the *Rule of St. Benedict* provides a tone for the whole community. Everyone knows the expectations and this has proven successful for thousands of years.

In our text Matthew continues to describe the common expectations for how Christians are to treat each other. Someone has called these expectations "household rules" for the family of faith. For Christians these "household rules" are intended to hold us together in mutual love and service. They transcend our diversity and differences. They have the same purpose as classroom expectations or an ancient monastic rule.

By the way, I think Christians sometimes get confused when others who are outside the family of faith don't play by the same rules that Christians do. We may wish that they did for any number of good reasons, but it is neither fair nor appropriate to expect those who are not Christians to live by rules to which they have not agreed. In the same way, the state is the state, and the church is the church. They are separate and the rules for each are different; to conflate them leads to confusion.

On the other hand, it's completely appropriate for Christians to expect certain things of each other because we hold these common household rules that are given in scripture.

Saint Paul summed it up this way: Be in debt to no one but to love one another. Judge not those who hold different opinions about matters of no consequence. Let your life be an offense to no one. Live mindfully before God who is the judge of the living and the dead.

In Matthew Jesus says: Hold one another accountable. If your brother or sister sins against you, go and speak directly to that person, so that he or she may be restored to newness of life. Do not tolerate what is intolerable.

Now this: Forgive those who sin against you. How many times? As many times as necessary.

Anyone who has tried to forgive can understand Peter's astonishment at Jesus' call to forgive, again and again and again. I find it terribly complex, and frankly impossible, to unfold neatly in a single sermon. Christians have been working on this since the beginning. Perhaps it is important to remember a story from the desert fathers of the sixth century.

Some brothers came to their abbot asking him to judge another who had committed some unnamed sin. The abbot refused, but they insisted. He relented. As he approached the nearby village, they could see that he had a wineskin on his back filled with sand that was pouring out behind him. They asked, "Abbot, why do you have this wineskin with sand pouring out?" He said, "You have asked me to come and judge the sins of another, and yet my sins are pouring out behind me." They were astonished and offered forgiveness to the their brother.

The moment you step along the path of forgiveness, some difficult questions arise.
- Do repeat offenders deserve to be forgiven?
- Does forgiveness encourage further abuse?
- Does forgiveness mean that I must forget the offense?
- What if someone doesn't ask to be forgiven?
- Doesn't forgiving just let people off the hook?
- Are some offenses just unforgivable?

These are serious questions that require serious conversation. The more deeply you have been offended, the more difficult forgiveness is. A petty insult is not the same as a marriage betrayal or a slain loved one. Forgiveness is always on a continuum. Yet no matter the offense, being unable (or unwilling) to forgive leaves you tangled up in misery, chained to the offense, and paralyzed from moving on to a new future. Jesus is asserting a whole new way of life for his followers by the radical act of forgiveness. On the one hand, forgiveness seems impossible; on the other hand, Jesus says it is essential. That is the way it is. How do we go forward into the future Jesus intends for his followers?

Christians have to begin, not with ourselves, but with the triune God who displays for us what it is to forgive. The astonishingly good news is that God came among us in Jesus, announcing the forgiveness of our sins and calling us to a new relationship with God and neighbor. He calls us to a new relationship made possible by the forgiveness of our sins in Jesus Christ. That is the center to which we always turn with grateful hearts. It begins with God's power and merciful desire to forgive us, not our power.

It's all about God's grace. I think this is the lesson of the abbot carrying the wineskin of sand.

It is only our experience of God's radical forgiveness in Jesus Christ, renewed every single day, that makes it possible to forgive those who hurt us. Christians have no other model than the triune God, and we have no other strength than the power of the Holy Spirit at work within us to do what is otherwise impossible.

When Jesus told Peter to forgive seventy times seven times, he was inviting him into a way of life with forgiveness at the center. It is this same way of life that you and I are invited to live. Forgiveness is a way of life that begins with the experience of God's forgiveness.

The process may last a lifetime but the alternative is worse. Anne Lamott famously said, "Refusing to forgive is like drinking rat poison and expecting the other person to die."[1]

I don't suggest for a moment that practicing forgiveness is easy. It is not any easier than loving our enemies. They are both impossible. Yet Jesus calls his followers to do both precisely so that I will not be the same as my enemy or forever chained to the one who has harmed me. We are unable to do the impossible, but with the strength of God at work within us, remarkable things do happen. The courage to act is the courage of the Holy Spirit at work within us. All that is required of us is to take the next right step in faithful obedience to Jesus' command.

Some wounds are deeper than others and require more work. Yet I am certain that freedom lies in surrendering those who have offended me unto God whose ways are mysterious and whose justice is as certain as it is merciful.

This is the way of freedom, and it is the Spirit of Christ at work within us that makes it possible. Perhaps this is why Saint Paul said, "I can do all things through Christ who strengthens me, even forgive the one who offends me" (Philippians 4:13).

Thanks be to God. Amen.

---

1. Anne Lamott, *Traveling Mercies: Some Thoughts on Faith* (New York: Pantheon Books, 1999).

Proper 20 / Pentecost 16 / Ordinary Time 25
Matthew 20:1-16

Beyond Fairness

I've run enough long-distance races to take joy in this passage — including the 200 mile Ragnar Relay; not *the first shall be last*; that has never been my burden, but *the last shall be first*. Now that gives me hope! As well it should even though I'm confident this parable has absolutely nothing to do with running or any other athletic endeavor, unless one considers gardening to be such. It should be noted too, for the sake of honesty, that I may well be misreading the parable by taking hope instead of judgment from it. After all, it's a cautionary tale aimed to remind those who arrive first that the permanency of their status is illusionary, and nothing in which to take pride. In fact, it's a warning for those who take umbrage at the ones who arrive late and do less work, and thus deserve less than the hardworking, early-to-rise, late-to-bed crowd.

The first shall be last and the last shall be first is a cautionary reminder indeed, but just what is it that Jesus wants us always to remember? There are those who suggest that the parable is another example of the generous grace of the landowner (God) overwhelming the expectations of the laborers. Perhaps.

Saint Paul would certainly approve of such a reading since he himself reminded us it is by grace that we are made whole, and it is not in our works that we earn our status before a loving God (Ephesians 2). In a mostly workaholic culture, one might think that his is the greatest news of all even though it overturns the notion that all the best things in life come to us by hard work. The greatest thing in our life actually comes as a gift from God, not as a reward for our work. That is an occasion for joy! But before we wrap up that package, we should note that there is no mention of the word grace in this parable, and there is certainly no denunciation of work implied, as if the hard work of the early risers were held against them in favor of those who worked less and received a reward. That would be a common misreading of the value of hard work over the abundance of grace. Binary thinking that divides reality into good versus bad creates a division that never gets us into the deeper truth.

Some suggest, and I am one of them, that the way to enter the parable is through the door in the opening phrase. *The kingdom of heaven is like a landowner.* That little phrase tips us off that this story is pointing us toward the reign of God on earth. The way God arranged things turned out to be quite a bit different than our normal ways of social arrangement. In the parable, those laborers who received exactly what was promised them at the beginning of the day turned resentful at the end of the day when the last chosen got precisely what they did because the landowner chose to be generous toward them. *It's not fair!* They cried. What is it about those of us who are *privileged* to be at the top of the social rung? From our position of privilege, we see life so differently than those who barely get by, whose lives are a struggle every waking hour. *But it's not fair*, we cry when the ones we've labeled undeserving actually get a place at the table. (We miss the irony of calling our fellow laborers *undeserving* because we live under the illusion that we deserve all the privileges we have accrued by our hard work, social pedigree and well-mannered living.) From this place of privilege — which is first place — it's impossible to see the way God arranges the world. No wonder the first shall be last: it appears to be the best position to see the generosity of God.

Take the border for instance. There are men and women who risk life and limb, even break the law, putting their lives in the hands of "coyotes" to carry them across a border in order that they may find work to support their families, most of whom are desperately poor. *It's not fair! Send them back. They are taking our jobs. They are breaking the law. Build a bigger, better fence. We built this country; they are freeloaders.*

Several congregations of Christians along the border of Texas have decided there is a different calculus to measure virtue. They began to view life from the perspective of those who are last, lost, and lonely. They began to imagine what it might be like to be desperate enough to send your children to a better life than your own. From that perspective, which is impossible to gain from a place of privilege, they began acting like Christians who know God is the landowner who is generous beyond all our calculations of fairness and whose justice is always shaped by mercy. The cry *it's not fair* was overcome by the glad sounds of the faithful singing, *welcome home; there is a place at table. Here is your water and here is your bed.*

There is a different kind of calculus at work when we begin to see life from the perspective of the landowner who chooses generosity and goodness toward all people.

The world of merit-based living teaches one thing — you get what you deserve as a result of your hard work. Certainly hard work is a good thing. There are rewards that come with hard work. Trust me, when you arrive at the finish line of a marathon, you know you have earned it by your training. We know all of this; but that's not the whole story. The privileged usually stop there with a great round of applause for our hard work. It's an illusion. You receive a great deal you didn't earn by hard work or can't buy with enough money. These are gifts of love, of friendship, of family, and of friends. Above all: the gift of abundant life in God. These are not earned or bought. They are given from the bounty of a generous God. The perspective of privilege can actually blind us from seeing such generosity.

When a labor pool operated not that far from here, men would stand for hours all day in the open air, waiting in hope for someone to select them for job. A truck would drive up and the men would scramble with hands raised, pleading to be selected. Each time a man climbed into the truck, there was joy spread across his face, along with relief. On the opposite side of the street stood people dressed as though they need not worry about such things, with cameras focused in expectant hope that one of those men might be arrested and be sent back across the border. They screamed hateful things, their faces distorted by anger and hatred. "You get what you deserve" produces life with a hard edge. It creates an angry people without mercy or compassion. The generosity of the landowner is constantly questioned or rejected. But have you noticed that the perspective of those who come last, who are welcomed home when they least expect it, are often filled with a sense of joy and gratitude?

Jonah cried: Lord, you can't save those people — those worthless, no good, undeserving, godless Ninevites! It's not fair. Why send me there to those people? God has a different plan for our lives.

The parable offers a different way than fairness and just desserts. God freely gives to *all* the riches of love. When we turn our attention away from ourselves toward God, we gaze upon one who is always making a place at the table, always widening the space for community, and always giving without regard to earning.

Here in this place without privilege, knowing ourselves as receivers of God's astonishing mercy is what opens wide our hearts to be merciful to others.

What is the take-home message? Because God is generous to us, we can be generous with others.

Amen.

Proper 21 / Pentecost 17 / Ordinary Time 26
Matthew 21:23-32

Words Are not Enough

It may be helpful when considering this text to remind ourselves that each of the gospel writers had a purpose in mind when writing the good news. They all shared a common purpose in telling the story of Jesus' life, death, and resurrection, but each had a particular community to which they were writing, and they shaped their gospel in ways peculiar to their listeners. That means we have to discern what the original intent of Matthew or Mark, Luke, or John, may have been and what that intent looks like today. This *interpretive discipline* is required not only for preachers; it is necessary for anyone who reads the gospel or any of the biblical texts with a hope to discover God's purpose today. The way of Christ that we seek does not fall out of the biblical text fully assembled, needing only to be plugged in, lit up, or turned on to go down the path. It's just not that easy.

Biblical texts, particularly the parables, require something more from us. They summon us to listen carefully and then make interpretive bridges from the land of their origin with its vineyards and fig trees, sheep and goats, to the land we live in that is vastly different, at least on the surface of things. People who listen for God's voice in the text and then risk living by what we believe to be truth, construct interpretive bridges. We all do it. Without that risk there is no bridge from the land of the origin to the land of our life today, which is to say that without risking ourselves on the gospel as we understand it, there is no Christian discipleship.

Then what is Matthew's peculiar purpose in writing his gospel? It can be summed up as *the moral formation of a people of faith gathered around their belief in Jesus as the saving one of God*. Matthew's gospel in particular has a moral earnestness that is deeply concerned that the gift of salvation we have been given issues forth in lives reflecting the way of the giver. There can be no separation of grace from ethics. The clearest example of this is the Sermon on the Mount that began with the Beatitudes followed by a description for practical living after the manner of Jesus. The scariest example may be the parable of the sheep and goats, where those who failed to recognize Jesus in the broken, battered, hungry, thirsty, and downtrodden and act with mercy, would be banished to outer darkness. Not a pretty picture especially for those who expect a gospel that is only about spiritual uplift or personal self-improvement. Not a pretty picture to have no claims that will change our lives if we live them well and form us into the people Jesus intended his disciples to be.

I, for one, don't find the parables of judgment to be easy going. They all scare me. I would rather avoid them altogether and not because I don't understand them. Mostly it is because I often find myself on the losing end, never measuring up, and left wondering how painful can it be to gnash my teeth for eternity. Remembering that Matthew's purpose is the moral formation of people gathered around Jesus helps enormously, though it doesn't fully reduce the tension. Maybe that is exactly what Matthew intended for his listeners: that the costly gift of God's salvation in Jesus would never be separated from the moral life that goes with being the followers of Jesus. To release the tension of grace and practice would cheapen the gift. That is why I think it is best *not* to avoid these difficult, easily misunderstood parables. There is enough pressure already to reduce the Christian faith into a personal entertainment program that rarely demands anything of us. Experiencing a little discomfort, even a lot of discomfort, when wrestling with the gospel is a good thing, especially when that discomfort drives us more deeply into the mercy of God, who has announced his saving intention for us in Jesus.

The parable before us asks a straightforward question: Which is better: for a son to say he is going to do something and not do it, or a son who initially says he is not going to do something, but then turns around and does it in the end? We know the answer. It's better to do the deed in the end than to say you will and then not follow through. Words of good intention are empty if they don't lead to action.

The religious leaders could not fathom Jesus as God's Messiah, the saving one who, after being baptized by John the Baptist, rose from the waters with God's voice echoing around him, "You are my beloved Son, in whom I am well-pleased." This Jesus who dared to judge their economic system by overturning their money tables and challenging the temple tax system, could not possibly be the saving one, promised by the John the Baptist. These learned religious leaders, who had all the words of scripture laid before them, could not accept that this Jesus was the saving one. Yet, those who had no words of promise uttered to them, no Messiah to claim — the outsiders, the sinners, and tax collectors, they are the ones who come streaming into the vineyard to claim Jesus as their saving one and follow him as the Lord of their lives. The leaders looked around at the signs of God's saving power in Jesus — the blind could see, the lame could leap, the wounded were healed, the outsiders were welcomed into the kingdom — and they utterly failed to see them as they were intended to be seen: the clues to God's dream being fulfilled in Jesus. So while the vineyard is their own, they failed to act on the words they were given.

What is the interpretive bridge from their land to our land? Surely, this is not only about a judgment on the religious leaders of Jesus' time. God is always at work among us. The question is whether you and I notice and take heed. Who is the saving one for us? Will our words lead to action?

For instance, I remain astonished by a story of two mothers, both grieving, who were featured in the *Washington Post*. One was wearing a big church hat, cradling the other on her shoulder. The one with the hat was grieving the loss of her teenage son who was murdered; the other was grieving the loss of her son, in prison for murdering the other mother's son. The mother of the murdered boy had forgiven the murderer and embraced his mother. They were praying for one another in their grief. That might be enough for most of us. But that mother, a deacon in her Baptist church, knew that *words were not enough*. She still travels from house-to-house between the warring housing projects that brought the death of her son, knocking on doors, and inviting people to be reconciled in the Spirit of Jesus. This is the vineyard of the Lord and she is doing her part to announce a better way by living a better way, the way of God's peace, forgiveness, and reconciliation.

The judgment of the parable is upon those who say one thing and do nothing about it. It is a necessary reminder for one who lives by words to acknowledge that words are sometimes not enough. When it comes to the work of the church, I have to ask myself repeatedly whether I am working in the vineyard of Lord or merely maintaining the institution that carries his name.

Whenever church work becomes focused on ensuring the survival of the institution, it loses its essential purpose. Where we want to be is in the vineyard of the world gladly announcing the good news that God has come among us in Jesus, bringing peace, forgiveness, and reconciliation — with words *and actions*.

The religious leaders were puzzled and ultimately furious because Jesus was overturning the institution they maintained. What Jesus knew is that institutions are transformed and remain vital when they stay focused on their essential purpose: announcing the good news of God's reconciling love for all people and especially the lost.

Amen.

Proper 22 / Pentecost 18 / Ordinary Time 27
Matthew 21:33-46

What Are We Protecting?

To say this parable is difficult to hear, much less interpret, is an understatement. To those who have ears to hear, it will make you wince and perhaps wish to throw up at the ending. But, listeners take heart: that very human reaction should not deter us from the considerable challenge of listening to this parable with the hope that we will be sufficiently unsettled to learn from it. In fact, Amy-Jill Levine, the Orthodox Jew who teaches New Testament at Vanderbilt University, argues that we should welcome the discomfort of the parables, particularly this one. Reminding us of Mark's comment that Jesus would speak only in parables (Mark 4:33-34), she says, "What makes the parables mysterious, or difficult, is that they challenge us to look into hidden aspects of our own values, our own lives.

They bring to the surface unasked questions, and they reveal answers we have always known, but refuse to acknowledge. Our reaction to them should be one of resistance rather than acceptance."[1] So, according to the wise professor, in the likely event that you are disturbed with many aspects of this particular parable of Jesus (including the graphic violence), resisting the surface level interpretation, then you are in a good posture to hear something more. Or you are in a posture at least to be challenged to discover something more than that which makes you comfortable — something that might cause you to think differently and, more importantly, act differently. The parables will do that to you.

The parables of Jesus are not told to provide general moral prescriptions or life lessons that can go on a bumper sticker. They are by nature difficult and demanding, open to multiple interpretations, each of which is unsettling to the hearer. Levine argues, "If we stop with the easy lessons, good though they may be, we lose the way Jesus' first followers would have heard the parables, and we lose the genius of Jesus' teaching. Those followers like Jesus himself, were Jews, and Jews knew that parables were more than children's stories or restatements of common knowledge. They knew that parables and the tellers of parables were there to prompt them to see the world in a different way, to challenge, and at times to indict."[2]

In the parable before us the setting is similar to previous parables in Matthew: a vineyard, a landowner, and tenants. (We should also note that it is borrowed from Isaiah 5:1-7 and would have been somewhat familiar to the original listener.) In the conventional Christian interpretation, this parable has been read as a justification for the replacement of God's people, Israel, by Jesus and his church. The doctrine of supersessionism is the pernicious belief that the coming of Jesus supersedes the people of Israel; hence the treatment of the slaves — beaten, stoned, and killed — reflects that of the Jewish establishment against Jesus and his followers. This turning of the parable into an allegory to justify a reading that has led to such terrible consequences for God's covenant people, and for Christians who perpetrate violence in the name of Jesus, forces us to a different reading — one that is fresh, historically accurate, and more likely to confront us with the truth. While the historical context is the rising confrontation between Jesus and the religious authorities who resist his new teaching and refuse to consider a new messenger of God's good news, the question is *how can we hear God's word to us through this confrontation?*

Are we simply to repeat the errors of Christian history by continuing the battles that Matthew's community had with the Jewish leaders of his time? They were in a contest as to who was the rightful interpreter of Torah and the coming of the Messiah. That contest has led to violent rhetoric and violence itself, neither of which is in keeping with Jesus' teaching, Matthew's vision, nor with what is necessary for today when efforts are made to understand the common roots of Judaism and Christianity.

For instance in light of the parable, we might place ourselves as the tenants of land given to us by the landowner. What precisely is it that the followers of Jesus have been asked to tend that belongs to another who has charged us with stewardship? This question moves us away from interpretations that merely perpetuate anti-Jewish sentiments toward one that forces us to consider our management of what has been entrusted to us and our treatment of those who claim to recover what belongs to God alone.

Perhaps those of us in the church consider ourselves to be entrusted with the true faith of the church, its doctrines, and the integrity of the gospel. God has given us such responsibility much like tenants over the land. It our solemn duty to do as instructed by the one who called us. This is true not only for priests and pastors, but also for all who rightly care about the integrity and truth of the Christian gospel. We consider ourselves charged with responsibilities that we hold sacred. One might think the current debates in the church are over just what this stewardship of the truth means and how it is being exercised today.

One pastor, Cynthia Jarvis, commenting on this possible way of reading the parable says, "As our minds are made up about the grasp we have on the truth as zealous guardians of the church's doctrines, the parable enrages us."[3] Why? It is because of our fierce insistence, not unlike the religious authorities of Jesus' time, that we now have the right religious answer over against all those who might come as messengers bringing God's good news in a fresh way. Jarvis argues that one way to read this parable is a contest between established religion, with all its rigid patterns, against revelation that breaks our patterns and reveals God's way among us. She writes, "The parable convicts us. Religious institutions function in most societies to conserve the beliefs, morals, and reigning social order. Priests of that order are reluctant to change their minds when confronted with a contrary witness to the truth — with a living word that invariably surprises them if it turns out, through the working of God's Spirit, to be God's word."[4]

On this reading of the parable, we who tend what belongs to God might ask ourselves more carefully if we are capable of hearing from messengers that confront us with their assertion of truthful revelation what makes us uncomfortable, disturbs our normal patterns, and causes us to rethink what we have always considered to be truth. How can we live as faithful stewards of what God has placed in our care — like the tenants — yet with an open heart and a mind that holds this responsibility lightly enough to welcome the messengers who come with unsettling news? As we approach the parable to hear something new, we might find that it speaks from a strange angle, one that provokes us to consider how we are living and to hear judgment if necessary.

In the parable, the son returns as a final gesture of the landowner. He is killed. That of course is the last straw. The Pharisees hear the truth about themselves, and their teeth are set on edge. The hammer, presumed to be that of God, will come down hard. But, what are we who look to Jesus Christ for our salvation to make of this judgment, especially if we do not point the finger easily at the Pharisees, but rather to ourselves who are now the guardians of the faith entrusted to us?

This is the turning point. Messengers, one after the other, come to us, bringing strange unsettling news about our stewardship; they speak in the name of God, and we resist them, sometimes forcibly, as occurs when the new light of revelation confronts received religion. We can and do beat the messenger. The parable suggests that the landowner is relentless in sending messengers against all odds and with great patience. The battered and beaten return with the bad news, and he keeps sending more messengers to those entrusted to care for the vineyard. It's as if he does not want to believe the tenants could be so tenacious in their resistance. We look at Christian history and notice the same thing has occurred from generation to generation.

Yet there may come a time when the Son — the living word of God — comes to us, confronts us, and calls us to a new understanding. That moment — and how we respond to it — will be the moment when this parable is fulfilled. If we have ears to hear, our rage and our conviction will be the moment the gospel comes alive for us.

Amen.

---

1. Amy-Jill Levine, *Short Stories by Jesus* (San Francisco: Harper/One, 2014).
2. *Ibid.*, p. 4.
3. Cynthia Jarvis, *Feasting on the Gospels* (Louisville: Westminster John Knox, 2014), p. 178.
4. *Ibid.*, p. 180.

www.ingramcontent.com/pod-product-compliance
Lightning Source LLC
Chambersburg PA
CBHW071757040426
42446CB00012B/2592